Pets on Jets

By Sascha Goddard

I bet you have met
lots of pets.

Do you think a pet could go on a jet?

Pets **do** get let on some jets!

Some pets sit in bags
to go on jets.

This cat is in a pet bag.

Some little pets sit on laps.

This pet gets a snack on the jet.

Some big pets must go
in a pet box to get on a jet.

This dog will go on a jet
that is just for pets!

Jet trips can be a big thing for pets.

They can get upset.

This man hugs his dog so it will not fret.

If **you** fret on jets, pets can help with that, too.

Kim's pet sits with her, so Kim will not fret.

So, can pets get on jets?

Yes!

Big pets and little pets
can get set and go!

CHECKING FOR MEANING

1. Which pet in the book was in a pet bag? *(Literal)*

2. Which pet in the book was in a pet box? *(Literal)*

3. Why might pets get upset when they go on a jet? *(Inferential)*

EXTENDING VOCABULARY

bet	What does the author mean when she says, *I bet you have met lots of pets*? Use *I bet* in a sentence of your own to show what it means.
trips	What does the word *trips* mean in the book? What else can *trips* mean?
fret	Look at the word *fret*. What does it mean? E.g. worry, stress, feel sad. Find three other words in the book that rhyme with *fret*. E.g. *jet, pet, bet*.

MOVING BEYOND THE TEXT

1. What kinds of pets might not be able to go on jets? Why?

2. How might larger animals be moved from one place to another?

3. What are some reasons why pets might need to go on jets?

4. If you could go anywhere on a jet, where would you choose? Why?

SPEED SOUNDS

| at | an | ap | et | og | ug |

| ell | ack | ash | ing |

PRACTICE WORDS

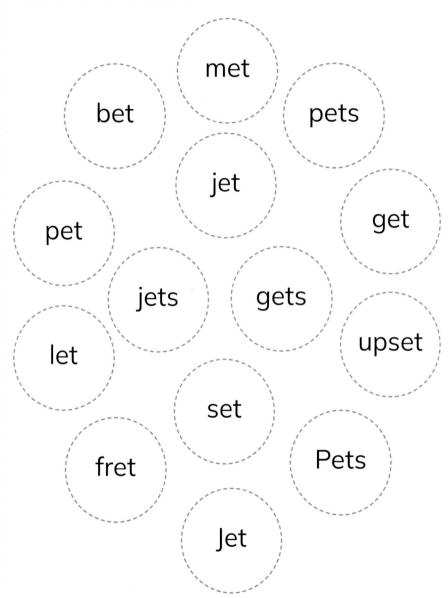

met

bet

pets

jet

pet

get

jets

gets

let

upset

set

fret

Pets

Jet